FEBRUARY 50 COLORING PAGES FOR ADULTS RELAXATION

SHIH CHIEN HUA

PUBLISHED BY:
SHIH CHIEN HUA
Copyright © 2018

SEABIRD SHOP >50FOR

FB FAN PAGE

Disclaimer
The information contained in this book is for general information purposes only. The information is provided by the authors and while we endeavor to keep the information up to date and correct, we make no representations or warranties of any kind, express or implied, about the completeness, accuracy, reliability, suitability or availability with respect to the book or the information, products, services, or related graphics contained in the book for any purpose. Any reliance you place on such information is therefore strictly at your own risk.

FEBRUARY 1ST

note:

_____

_____

_____

FEBRUARY 2ND

note:

_____

_____

_____

FEBRUARY 3RD

note:

_____

_____

_____

FEBRUARY 4TH

note:

_____

_____

_____

FEBRUARY 5TH

note:

_____

_____

_____

FEBRUARY 6TH

note:

_____

_____

_____

FEBRUARY 7TH

note:

_____

_____

_____

FEBRUARY 8TH

note:

_____

_____

_____

FEBRUARY 9TH

note:

_____

_____

_____

FEBRUARY 10TH

note:

_____

_____

_____

FEBRUARY 11TH

note:

_____

_____

_____

FEBRUARY 12TH

note:

_____

_____

_____

FEBRUARY 13TH

note:

_____

_____

_____

FEBRUARY 14TH

note:

_____

_____

_____

FEBRUARY 15TH

note:

_____

_____

_____

FEBRUARY 16TH

note:

_____

_____

_____

FEBRUARY 17TH

note:

_____

_____

_____

FEBRUARY 18TH

note:

_____

_____

_____

FEBRUARY 19TH

note:

_____

_____

_____

FEBRUARY 20TH

note:

_____

_____

_____

FEBRUARY 21TH

note:

_____

_____

_____

FEBRUARY 22TH

note:

_____

_____

_____

FEBRUARY 23TH

note:

_____

_____

_____

FEBRUARY 24TH

note:

_____

_____

_____

FEBRUARY 25TH

note:

_____

_____

_____

FEBRUARY 26TH

note:

_____

_____

_____

FEBRUARY 27TH

note:

_____

_____

_____

FEBRUARY 28TH

note:

_____

_____

_____

FEBRUARY 29TH

note:

_____

_____

_____

FEBRUARY 30TH

note:

_____

_____

_____

FEBRUARY 31TH

note:

_____

_____

_____

FEBRUARY 32TH

note:

_____

_____

_____

FEBRUARY 33TH

note:

_____

_____

_____

FEBRUARY 34TH

note:

_____

_____

_____

FEBRUARY 35TH

note:

_____

_____

_____

FEBRUARY 36TH

note:

_____

_____

_____

FEBRUARY 37TH

note:

_____

_____

_____

FEBRUARY 38TH

note:

_____

_____

_____

FEBRUARY 39TH

note:

_____

_____

_____

FEBRUARY 40TH

note:

_____

_____

_____

FEBRUARY 4TH

note:

_____

_____

_____

FEBRUARY 42TH

note:

_____

_____

_____

FEBRUARY 43TH

note:

_____

_____

_____

FEBRUARY 44TH

note:

_____

_____

_____

FEBRUARY 45TH

note:

_____

_____

_____

FEBRUARY 46TH

note:

_____

_____

_____

FEBRUARY 47TH

note:

_____

_____

_____

FEBRUARY 48TH

note:

_____

_____

_____

FEBRUARY 49TH

note:

_____

_____

_____

FEBRUARY 50TH

note:

_____

_____

_____